Genre ▶ Historical F

MW00675590

? **Essential Question**
How do traditions connect people?

Maple Sugar Moon

by Cheryl Minnema
Mille Lacs Band of Ojibwe
Illustrated by Kristina Rodanas

Chapter 1
Waiting. 2

Chapter 2
Best Friends. 5

Chapter 3
The Sound of the Aandeg. 8

Chapter 4
Maple Sugar Camp 12

Respond to Reading. 16

PAIRED READ Maple Sugar. 17

Focus on Genre. 20

Chapter 1
Waiting

On a cold March day in 1864, Omadwe and her dog Bezhig looked out between the trees at the snow-covered field. The field was as empty as her stomach. There was no sign of the hunters who had left the village three days ago. Omadwe turned back and followed her shallow gray footprints towards the village of snow-covered wigwams. Her stomach tightened with a growl. "I don't know about you Bezhig, but I'm hungry."

Bezhig wagged his tail at the sound of her voice, his tongue flapping beneath his frosted breaths.

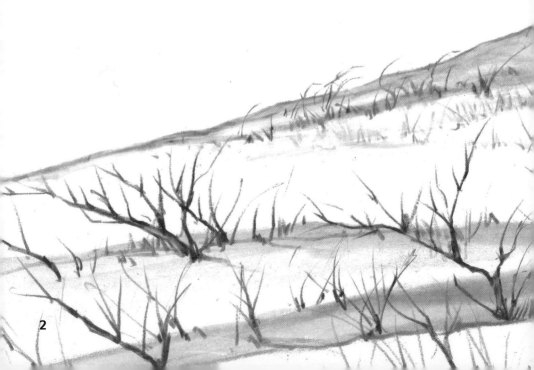

It had been a long winter with little meat. In the last decade, settlers had taken land that was part of the Fond du Lac reservation. This meant less land for hunting.

The settlers had hired young men from the reservation to cut down trees. This winter, many young men had been hurt cutting trees. One had even died.

Only five hunters were left in the village. One of them was Omadwe's father, Young Kegg. Omadwe had watched her father get ready for the hunting trip. He had his new hatchet. He had traded with the settlers for it.

"The settlers are changing the ways of our ancestors," said Omadewe. "They took our land. Now they want us be like them."

Young Kegg hugged Omadwe and said, "We're the People. We will not let them take our ways."

STOP AND CHECK

What has the winter been like for Omadwe's village?

Chapter 2
Best Friends

Remembering her father's words, Omadwe rubbed her stomach. The pain in her stomach wasn't just from hunger. What if her father did not come back? In January, her best friend Zhaawan's father had died in an accident. He'd been cutting trees for the settlers. The intensity of Omadwe's fear made her stomach hurt.

Zhaawan had been her best friend. But last fall, Zhaawan insisted on being called "Angelina." In October, Zhaawan and her family moved from their wigwam into a wooden house. Then, Zhaawan began criticizing Omadwe's clothes.

"I don't know why you wear those dirty leather scraps," Zhaawan would say as she admired her own new blue cotton dress. "Your father could trade furs for a dress like mine."

Omadwe had ignored her after that. But Omadwe missed her friend who had become Angelina.

After her father died, Zhaawan and her mother had moved in with her father's family. Zhaawan rarely left her grandmother's wigwam. This surprised Omadwe. She thought Zhaawan loved living in the wooden house. Omadwe wondered if she was wrong about her friend.

Suddenly, Bezhig bolted after a waabooz (rabbit) and was gone.

"Bezhig! Wait!" called Omadwe, but he didn't stop. Bezhig did not have the speed or endurance to catch the waabooz. He'd soon forfeit the chase and come back.

The cawing sound of an aandeg (crow) reached her ears. Hearing the aandeg was an honor. It was the first sign of maple sugaring season!

Chapter 3
The Sound of the Aandeg

Excited, Omadwe ran through the woods with Bezhig to share the news. She heard noise coming from the village. Had they already heard the sound of the aandeg?

Omadwe ran into the village and saw her father. He had a deer. The other hunters had rabbits. She ran to her father, thanking the Great Spirit for bringing the hunters home safely.

As Omadwe hugged her father, she remembered the cawing of the crows and shouted, "I heard the aandeg!"

A few days later, Omadwe was in the wigwam rolling up cattail mats when her mother, Ikwe, handed her some pouches.

"Put these outside with the food supply."

Omadwe took the leather pouches and opened the flap of the wigwam. On the ground by the door were four new pairs of snowshoes. She looked back at her mother with a big smile.

"We'll be going to the maple sugar camp today," said her mother.

"But why four pairs?" asked Omadwe.

"Zhaawan will be joining us this year," replied her mother.

Omadwe put the pouches by the food supply. She was glad that Zhaawan would be coming with them.

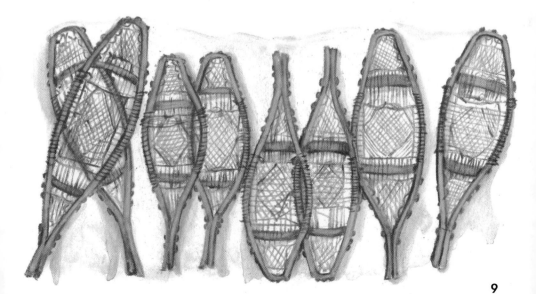

Later, as Omadwe walked with her parents through the village, she wondered how Zhaawan would be.

At the edge of the village, Omadewe saw Zhaawan peek out of her grandma's wigwam. Then she slowly stepped out wearing her old buckskin dress.

"Aaniin (Hi) Angelina," said Omadwe.

Zhaawan took a deep breath. "Please don't call me Angelina. I'm sorry for being mean to you," she said.

"You're my friend, always," Omadwe said and hugged her. Then she helped Zhaawan lace up her snowshoes.

STOP AND CHECK

How has Zhaawan changed since her father died?

Chapter 4
Maple Sugar Camp

After traveling all day, they reached the maple sugar camp. Young Kegg pounded the hatchet into a few maples. Then he put wooden spouts in the trees. Omadwe and Zhaawan placed birch bark baskets under each spout while Ikwe set up their camp. Unable to wait for the baskets to fill up, the girls each lay underneath a spout.

"Mmmm," said Omadwe.

Before Zhaawan could get a taste, Bezhig began licking her face. Zhaawan despised it when the dog licked her face. "Gego! (Don't) You're so irritating!" said Zhaawan. Omadwe laughed.

As darkness fell, Young Kegg made a fire. After a dinner of wild rice and deer meat, Omadwe and Zhaawan settled into the wigwam and fell asleep.

In the morning, Zhaawan gave Omadwe a necklace of shiny red beads. "I traded my blue dress for it," said Zhaawan.

"But you loved that dress," replied Omadwe.

Zhaawan hugged her. "I don't want anything that reminds me of the settlers. My father died working for them. Please take the necklace," she said.

All morning, Omadwe and Zhaawan gathered wood for the fire. Then they emptied the birch bark containers under the spouts. Next it was time to boil the maple water into syrup.

Young Kegg poured the sap water into the kettle and Ikwe began to stir it with a smooth wooden paddle. Each time it was about to boil over, Omadwe stirred the water with a pine branch. Zhaawan was amazed at how the bubbling foam retreated as soon as the pine branch touched it.

In the evening, the girls ate wild rice, deer meat, and hard maple candy.

"Look," Zhaawan said pointing at the full moon. "It's a maple sugar moon!" Omadwe laughed, happy that Zhaawan was here to share her joy during maple sugar time.

STOP AND CHECK

How do Omadwe and her family make maple syrup?

Summarize

Use the most important details from *Maple Sugar Moon* to summarize the story. Your graphic organizer may help.

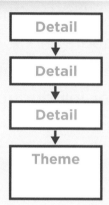

Detail
Detail
Detail
Theme

Text Evidence

1. How is this story an example of historical fiction? GENRE

2. How does Omadwe's father make her feel better about the settlers? THEME

3. What does *scraps* on page 6 mean? What does the word make you think of? Why do you think Zhaawan describes Omadwe's clothing in this way? CONNOTATION AND DENOTATION

4. Write about why Omadwe is excited to hear the crows and what maple sugar camp means to her. Use details from the text in your answer. WRITE ABOUT READING

Compare Texts

Read about the real-life inspiration for Omadwe and her story.

Maple Sugar

This story of *Maple Sugar Moon* was inspired by my Ojibwe grandmother, Lucy Kegg Clark (1901–1994). Her Ojibwe name was Omadwebigaashiikwe (the sound of waves coming onto the shore), but she was called Omadwe for short. Her parents were named Young Kegg and Chi ikwe zan(s).

A metal spout and bucket are used to collect sap from a maple tree.

Omadwe told many stories of traveling to the maple sugar camp in Minnesota to harvest maple sugar. She went with her parents and other family members. In these stories there was always a dog popping up somewhere.

Veronique St-Amand/iStock/Getty Images

This photograph was taken in 1908. It shows a Native American woman with birch bark baskets used for collecting sap.

Roland Reed/Buyenlarge/Archive Photos/Getty Images

In *Maple Sugar Moon,* the dog's name is Bezhig, which means "one." I have also included a few other Ojibwe words in the story like *waabooz* (rabbit) and *aandeg* (crow).

Omadwe was always hesitant about modern inventions, often trying a few new ways of doing things, but then quickly resorting to the traditional way.

To make maple sugar, the sap from the maple trees had to be harvested in the spring. A tap or spout was put in the tree to drain the sap. Birch bark baskets were used to collect it. The sap was boiled for hours until it turned into a thick syrup and then eventually turned to sugar. It was a lot of hard work. It took 40 gallons of sap to make just one gallon of maple syrup!

Make Connections

Why do you think the author wanted to write about her grandmother? ESSENTIAL QUESTION

How does "Maple Sugar" help you understand why Omadwe is excited to go to the maple sugar camp in *Maple Sugar Moon*? TEXT TO TEXT

Focus on Genre

Historical Fiction Historical fiction tells a made-up story that is set in the past. However, it often gives information about a real event and can show real people who were living at the time. Historical fiction gives the reader an understanding of life long ago.

Read and Find *Maple Sugar Moon* is not a true story, but it is based on the author's grandmother and some real events in her life. Explain which parts of the story are fact and which are fiction.

Your Turn

Native Americans have a tradition of telling familiar stories aloud. The stories tell about the past and keep their culture alive. Choose a person or an event in your family that you could tell a story about. You can make up some details to add interest, but base your story on key facts. Have your family give feedback on the story. Practice telling your story until it sounds and feels right. Then share it with others.